A BOOK OF HUMOROUS

POEMS

by

KEN KELSEY

K J Kelsey
kelsey@talk21.com

Cover design
Jo Kelsey
Jo1208@hotmail.com

CONTENTS

Rebecca Bagley

Dreams for Sale

COWBOY BUILDERS

Really, Mrs. Palmer, there's no need to make a drama
Of the one or two mishaps that have beset us.
They happen every day in a disconcerting way,
But we professionals must make sure they don't upset us.

Now the driver has said sorry that he backed his heavy lorry
Hard into the side of your Mercedes;
But I'm sure that you misheard that he said the effing word,
For he'd never use such terms in front of ladies.

And it wasn't all his fault that his nearside mirror caught
The slack in your satellite dish cable;
And from the ease with which it fell I could very quickly tell
That its fixing on the roof was quite unstable.

Since for that we're not to blame, I think that you should claim
On your insurance, and I'm as sure as hell
You'd recover all the cost of the many tiles you've lost -
Plus, of course, the greenhouse roof as well.

I'm sorry your cat came far too near our blow-torch flame
And suffered all that singeing to his rear;
And with one shrieking yell like a bat from out of hell
Shot through the door to get away from here.

As he left in such a hurry I don't think you need worry,
For his speed suggests that he is fit and sound.
You'll find his fur will grow within a month or so -
That is, of course, if he is ever found.

Now about the toxic bond we spilled in your garden pond
Where your specimen koi carp are being bred,
Though the water's turning brown and they're floating upside-
down,
Are you sure that means they're definitely dead?

Well, that only goes to show that we never really know
What lies ahead of us around the corner.
Of course, I'm only guessing, but I think it was a blessing
That at least it made the water that much warmer.

I'm so glad, Mrs. Palmer, that those pills have made you calmer.
For a while back there I thought you'd have a seizure
When our steam-and-strip machine vaporized your TV screen
And somehow blew the fuse in your fridge-freezer.

It's a shame it's all defrosted and will have to be composted,
Though you could of course give some of it away.
To help you out we'll take the brisket, 'cos we're quite prepared to risk it,
And then we really must be on our way.

I'll let my guv'nor know in the coming week or so
That on the whole you're not too satisfied
With some of what we've done, and I'm sure he'll be the one
To see your bill is duly rectified.

We'll be off now, Mrs. P, and it's heartening to see
That your neighbours will support you anyhow.
Though we've had our little frights things will soon be put to rights
For I think I hear the engines coming now.

* * *

SID's REVENGE

In a quiet suburban avenue
There lived a quite outrageous shrew.
Her husband, Sid, did all the chores,
The cooking, cleaning, hoovering floors.
From dawn to dusk he daily worked,
And woe betide him if he shirked.
His many tasks were itemised
On worksheets she had organised,
And as each irksome job was done
He'd mark it off, then carry on,
While she, a medium, would try
To reach dead friends from days gone by.
Sid suffered all her phony trances,
Her dreadful friends, their weird séances,
Once being banished to the shed
While they tried to contact Uncle Fred.
Alas! One day, I'm sad to say,
Poor henpecked Sid just passed away.
Our sorrow, though, gave way to laughter
When his will was read a few days after.

"Dear wife," it read, "For what it's worth,
You made my life a hell on earth.
But nonetheless I leave to you
All I possess, the work-sheets, too.
But first, there's something you should know;
That at our bank, some time ago,
I drew out all our cash, the lot,
And in some safe secluded spot
I buried it. But never fear,
Here's how to get it back, my dear.
Take my work-sheets - though now they're yours -
And every day do all the chores
Which you yourself said must be done.
So do them all - yes, every one -
And properly, mind! I'll have no botching!
Remember always I'll be watching!
When you've done that for one whole year
Just contact me, I'm bound to hear.
I'll tell you then just where it's hid.
Till then, bye bye,
Yours truly,
Sid."

* * *

STEPHEN'S STAG NIGHT

Stephen's stag night in the Strand
Rapidly got out of hand,
Resulting in unruly brawls
And one or two 999 calls.

The police came quickly on the scene
And stepped in close to intervene,
When Stephen, aiming random blows,
Struck a policeman on the nose.

Now you don't have to go to college
To acquire the common knowledge
That anyone who strikes a copper
Is bound to come a dreadful cropper.

So Stephen, far the worse for drink,
Spent the night in the nearby clink,
Brought next day before the beak
And remanded in custody for a week.

Panic gripped the hapless Steve
Who knew his bride-to-be would grieve
If instead of wedding bells
She'd hear him sobbing in the cells.

The magistrate heard his plaintive plea
And, anxious to show charity,
By way of nuptial contribution
Granted a stay of execution.

Steve and escort sped off apace
To where the wedding would take place;
No time to change, no time to care,
They made it with no time to spare.

So, handcuffed to a tall young copper,
Which all the guests thought most improper,
Steve stood waiting by the aisle
Longing to see his true love's smile.

The bride-to-be arrived at last
And looked at Steve, her groom, aghast;
Unkempt, dishevelled, crumpled, grubby,
Handcuffed to a handsome bobby.

She met the young policeman's eyes
And in a moment of surprise
Each knew that one of Cupid's darts
Had pierced their unsuspecting hearts.

Then, as the ceremony progressed
The young policeman grew obsessed,
And when the vicar asked, "Do you....?"
He cried aloud, "*I* do! *I* do!"

As Stephen languishes in his cell
His erstwhile bride fares very well
Within two strong arms of the law
And thinks of luckless Steve no more.

* * *

EMILY PRINGLE

What were you thinking, Emily Pringle,
Thirty years plus and depressingly single,
As you sat in the computer room at the Bank
Paid less than the others in spite of your rank?
What were you thinking as you faced the screen?
Were you pondering upon what life might have been
Had you managed to find a presentable gent
Who'd tell you he loved you and helped pay the rent?
As you spent your whole day monitoring meaningless figures,
Trying hard to ignore the younger girls' sniggers,
Did you ask yourself ever, "Is it all worth it?
If it all ended now, what would I forfeit?"
What did you think on that unhappy day
When they gave you a cheque for redundancy pay?
As you dabbed your eyes with your Kleenex tissue
Did you know that next day no-one would miss you?

What now are you thinking, Emily Pringle?
Does the thought of the risks you took make your skin tingle?
But you're Amelie du Près now, whom everyone knows
As a frequent attender at top fashion shows.
You've a string of boutiques in New York and Milan,
Paris and Frankfurt, Dubai and Japan.
You've a range of cosmetics, so it's safe to assume
That soon you will launch your own brand of perfume.
Do you smile to yourself at the security flaws
Which you saw and exploited to make millions yours,
Transferring sums of increasing amounts
To one or another of your numbered accounts?
Just how many millions did you spirit off-shore?
Was it forty or fifty, or perhaps even more?
Good luck to you, Amelie, though I think you should know
That you're high on the list at the S.F.O.

* * *

THE CHECK-UP

You can get dressed now, and when you've done that
Come sit over here and we'll have a quiet chat.
I'm pleased at the way you are coming along.
Your pulse is quite steady, your heart-beat is strong.
One-four-five over eighty, not bad for your age;
No need for tablets, no, not at this stage.
I see from the screen you've a touch of angina;
No major threat, that, nor yet is it minor.
You still must keep active; brisk walking is best.
The knack is to know when to stop, when to rest.
You say you get breathless when climbing the stair.
At your time of life you must take extra care.
Now, we both know the cause, so once again, please,
You must lose some weight - it's not fair on your knees!
Cut down on all fats, salt, sugar and eggs.
Losing weight will diminish the pain in your legs.
Drink cod liver oil; it could ease your arthritis.
I'll give you some pills to relieve your cystitis.
Are you sleeping OK? You get cramp at night.
Well, try wearing socks, but make sure they're not tight.
By and large (no offence!) you're in pretty good nick.
I've seen far worse cases when tending the sick!
As long as you're careful I'm willing to bet
You've a good many years still in front of you yet.
I can reassure you, you've little to fear
So good-bye and God bless, till I see you next year.

She liked that young doctor - a wonderful bloke.
She was ever so sad when he died of a stroke.

* * *

BISCUITS

It was lunch-time in the City and the coffee bar looked pretty
So I put my drink and biscuits on a table.
In front of me there sat just an ordinary looking chap.
We ignored each other as far as we were able.
I opened up my Times to gen up on all the crimes
When he leaned across and to my great surprise
Opened up my biscuit pack, took one out and then sat back
And scoffed it up before my very eyes.
What's a chap supposed to do when faced with such a coup?
And even though I strenuously deplored it,
Being British through and through on my inner strength I drew
And determinedly but stoicly ignored it.
However, one must fight to assert one's legal rights,
So I demonstrably took a biscuit from the pack,
Then drew the packet nearer to make ownership much clearer,
Hoping that would stop the bounder in his tracks.
My hopes were all in vain as he leaned across again
And took out a petit buerre as I recall.
So not to be outdone *I* took another one,
Signalling my distaste at his great gall.
That was not, alas, the end, as my predatorial friend
Continued his encroachment on my wares.
This tit for tat went on till with all eight biscuits gone,
He got up and left, 'mid castigating glares.
Once he had departed I was eager to get started
On the crossword near the sports page at the back.
I flicked through each page to see, when there in front of me
Were my biscuits, yes, the whole unopened pack!

I think it is a pity that somewhere in the City
Is a chap whose jaundiced view of me is grim.
His judgement's right, of course; and I often feel remorse
That once I thought the very same of him.

* * *

THE TRAMP

I'll never forget the old fellow I met
In the store where we do all our shopping.
I could tell at a glance from his lopsided stance
That he was in grave danger of flopping.

He was stood very still near the queue by the till
Which gave me the chance to peruse
The way he was dressed from his jacket - unpressed -
Down to his scruffy old shoes.

His shoulders were stooped, his eyelids had drooped,
The personification of boredom;
His cuffs were both frayed and his trousers displayed
Every sign that some rodent had gnawed 'em.

I could tell his back ached by the way his frame quaked
From the weight of the bags he was carrying.
He looked so forlorn, so woebegone,
I found the whole scene very harrowing.

Though it's not quite my fashion I felt true compassion
T'wards this battered and tattered old tramp,
Being forced there to stand with no seating at hand,
In a posture conducive to cramp.

So by way of a greeting I gave him a fleeting
But sociable nod of my head.
By way of response he nodded *his* bonce;
Simultaneously, let it be said.

Delayed recognition made me doubt my decision,
So I stepped one pace forward to see,
I looked into his eyes and to my surprise
Saw the chap in the mirror was me!

* * *

WENDY'S WEDDING

Life has many gifts to offer
From its over-flowing coffer,
Which makes it difficult to measure
What constitutes the greatest treasure,
But the passing years have taught us
That high on the list are our granddaughters;
So when Wendy asked me if I'd say
Some words upon her wedding day
I was beside myself with pride
Although I knew deep down inside
I lacked the required inspiration
To find words fitting the occasion

Though on occasions such as these
I know it's customary to tease,
I ruled out telling family jokes
Which would be lost on other folks.
My grandsons I could tease with joy.
For each at heart remains a boy.
Rough banter's fine for blokes, that's plain,
But that's not how you handle porcelain.
Besides, words can often seem unkind
And stay a long time in the mind.
Furthermore there was no way
I'd mess things up on Wendy's day.

I must confess that once or twice
I thought of tendering some advice,
But then a voice inside me said,
"Get that notion out of your head!
The world you knew is in the past.
Times are changed and still changing fast.

Your own experiences, though great,
Are well beyond their sell-by date
And not relevant for the times to come.
Today's feet march to a different drum,
With a beat too fast for your tired old legs.
So don't tell your granddaughter how to suck eggs!"

So after a multitude of toasts
To bridesmaids, in-laws, guests and hosts,
I cautiously rose to say my part
And told them what was in my heart.
I began with an important point to make –
Indeed, the icing on the wedding cake –
That Wendy had shown exquisite taste
In choosing Simon as her mate,
The sort that any aspiring bride
Would like forever by her side.
And as they journeyed on through life,
A perfect couple, man and wife,
Sampling all of life's great riches
They'd carry all our loving wishes;
And as and when push came to shove
They could always rely on our boundless love.

I own that I was quite relieved
When my little speech was well-received
For with all the speeches there delivered
Mine was the only voice that quivered,
And when Wendy smiled and blew a kiss,
I knew I'd said nothing too amiss.
When the tables had all been cleared
And the waiting-staff had disappeared
We all assembled for the dance.
I gave the ballroom a casual glance
Then slipped away to take my ease
With all the other OAPs.

As the evening drew to a close
Wendy and Simon in travelling clothes
Came down to bid a fond adieu
To all their guests, and threaded through
The clamouring, joyful, loving throng,
And slowly made their way along,
Eventually reaching where I stood.
She hugged me as I knew she would,
Then touched my cheek and softly said,
"God bless you, Gramps," and then was led
By Simon to their waiting carriage
At the start I know of a loving marriage.

In joy we saw them both depart
But I'd mixed feelings in my heart,
Sadder than anyone there supposed.
My storybook of joy and dread
Has unknown pages yet unread
But I'd just seen another chapter closed.

* * *

GIRLS' DAY OUT

We went up to London, Meg, Molly and me.
The fare was expensive - our spirits were free.
We saw the prize sculptures on view at the Tate.
Well! If they call that art we must forcefully state
We don't know about art but we know what we hate,
  Do Meg, Molly and me.

We went into Harrods, me, Molly and Meg
Who tried on a coat which she took off the peg.
"It suits you divinely," the sales-lady purred,
"And at six hundred pounds the price is absurd!"
A thought, I confess, which had also occurred
  To me, Molly and Meg.

We went to a matinee, Meg, me and Molly.
The audience, all oldies, were lively and jolly.
Awaiting the curtain they had lots to say
About gardens and grandsons and going away.
"Reminds me a bit of our own U3A,"
  Thought Meg, me and Molly.

We rode back to Dorking, Meg, Molly and me,
With feet and sides aching, content as could be.
We said our goodbyes then went separate ways
To watch the TV with our suppers on trays,
Alone but not lonely. We treasure these days,
  Do Meg, Molly and me.

* * *

THE ARSONIST

This is the tale of Jasper Sly,
A seemingly unlucky guy,
Who nonetheless was unperturbed
By the fires which oft occurred
Destroying all the furs and gowns
He held in stock in various towns;
For after each successive claim
It seemed the richer he became.

For instance, he was on a cruise
When they broke to him the dreadful news;
But on returning from his hols
He bought himself a brand new Rolls.
Another time he wept aloud
As the Fire Brigade kept back the crowd;
But his smile was bright and his eyes were dry
When he bought more shares in ICI.

His house in Golders Green, though brash,
Was bought entirely with the cash
Donated by the Pearl, the Pru,
Lloyd's, Sun Alliance and NFU.
But Jasper erred in tempting Fate
Which, unbeknown had fixed the date
This arsonist of rag-trade premises
Would meet, unrecognised, his Nemesis.

So enters Percy, a genial soul,
Who chose to supplement his dole
By working as a part-time barman,
Roofer, cleaner, labourer, carman,
Receiving as his normal fee
Cash in hand and all tax-free,
Income he'd have not enjoyed
Were he not fully unemployed.

His many skills he advertised
On bits of paper, post-card sized,
Which Old Patel put on display
In his newsagent's window for 5p a day.
"Experienced roofer. Terms agreed.
Satisfaction guaranteed.
If your garage roof's a'leaking
I'm the craftsman you are seeking."

And so it was, as if by chance,
That Jasper gave that ad a glance,
And as the rain was coming through
His garage roof, without ado
He phoned to Percy who agreed
To do the job with utmost speed.
So mid-way through the following week
Percy arrived to tackle the leak.

After off-loading the burner and felt
And waiting around for the asphalt to melt,
He then read the Mirror and finished a fag
By which time his energy had started to flag.
Deciding the cause was his need for some grub
He climbed into his van and drove off to the pub;
There to indulge in the food he loved most -
Baked beans piled high upon pieces of toast.

His predilection for baked beans,
Acquired while he was in his teens,
This day was pre-ordained to be
The cause of untold misery;
For instead of being grateful
For a single piled-high plateful
He to the passing waitress beckoned
And rashly ordered up a second.
Then proceeding a la carte
Devoured a wedge of rhubarb tart,
And brought his repast to a finish
By downing yet another Guinness.

His far from balanced meal now ended
He drove back to Jasper's with stomach distended,
And as the afternoon progressed
Became increasingly distressed.

He could not work with belly so bloated
Nor with the discomfort which this promoted,
And soon the rumblings in his tum
Convinced him that the time had come
To seek de-pressurised relief;
So, tensing his muscles and clenching his teeth,
By a prolonged but natural function
He released the by-product of his gaseous luncheon.

This methane, searching for the air,
Found an outlet nearby where
His trusty blow-torch stood alight
Which caused the methane to ignite.
The flame pursued its natural course
And journeyed swiftly to the source,
Thereby scorching, inter alia,
His unsuspecting genitalia.

Poor Percy doubled up with pain,
Which caused him to break wind again,
So unwittingly infringeing
The patent for a two-stroke engine.
As the flames took hold he could not bear
Such novel thermal underwear,
So now with trousers well alight
He vainly sought relief in flight.

Into the house he headlong rushed,
His cheeks by now both hotly flushed,
And in his mind a single thought - t'
Plunge his bum in cooling water.
Flinging wide the kitchen door
He saw arranged upon the floor
Some thinners stored in pots and pans,
All part of Jasper's future plans.

Believing it was H_2O
He sat in one, which in a mo
Converted his ill-judged compulsion
Into a form of jet-propulsion.
For now like a doodle-bug he flew,
Through the ceiling, past the loo,
Defying laws once held inviolate
As, flying blind on auto pilot,

He blazed along the upstairs landing,
Then, stud-partition notwithstanding,
Crashed through into the master bedroom
Which, by virtue of its vaster headroom,
Allowed his progress aerobatic
To proceed unhindered t'wards the attic,
Ever onwards and upwards hurling,
Till brought to rest by a timber purlin.

Alas, poor Percy's now departed,
Leaving kinfolk broken-hearted,
Unable fully to comprehend
How he came to have such a fiery end.

The net result of Percy's flight
Was to set Jasper's house alight,
In the process leaving traces
Of thinners in unlikely places,
A fact which those with expertise
Could spot with unaccustomed ease.
A fact which also, at a guess,
Could lead to charges - but I digress.

The scene now shifts to Kingsland Road
Where Jasper had started to unload
Some cotton waste he planned to use
As a tried and trusted fuse,
When down the road with siren blaring
A police patrol car came a'tearing,
And from these policemen Jasper learned
That his house at Golders Green had burned.

This news invoked surprise, and sorrow,
For the fire was not until the morrow,
And not at his own private dwelling
But at his shop where the clothes weren't selling.
For a moment he stood there, stunned,
Mobile features moribund.
Then, unaware of Percy's fate
He started to expostulate.

"The roofer did it! God, he's dim!
I take it you have questioned him?"
"We cannot, sir, and I'll tell you why;
He's joined the dole queue in the sky.
But it was not him, and that's a fact,
For the garage roof is still intact.
No, this fire was started flagrantly
And caused by human agency.

"Which brings us to our own pet theory,
Prompting an initial query.
Can I ask you, for beginners,
Just why you needed all them thinners?"
Jasper sensed the situation,
Fraught with fearful implication,
Then as each ominous omen clicked
He heard the dreaded words "You're nicked!"

So, just as Fate had had in store,
Jasper now faced a Court of Law,
Incensed that he was being fitted
For a crime he'd not committed.
He really didn't have a prayer,
Not with "them thinners" everywhere.
But his fate was sealed beyond a doubt
When the record of his claims came out.

Hearing evidence so substantial,
Albeit mainly circumstantial,
The jury had no other choice
But to return with single voice
A "guilty" verdict. And so the beak
In passing sentence chose to speak
Of Jasper's many arsons past,
And hoped that this would be his last;
And since he gave him fifteen years
That's less naive than first appears.

Imprisoned now in Wormwood Scrubs
Jasper ponders Fate's cruel rub.
Despite his being not to blame
He'd lost his house but could not claim
And, shattering his equilibrium,
He'd only just renewed the premium.
In tears he agonises nightly
That he was wrongly wronged. Nay, rightly!
For when guilty he was quite content
For the world to deem him innocent.
Espousing values so perverse
Entails accepting the reverse.

So, gentle readers, shed no tears
O'er his imprisonment for years.
What's more, up there, our Percy waits
Beside St Peter's pearly gates,
Bedecked in his celestial raiment
And bent upon exacting payment.
With blow-torch lit and in his hand
His course of action's neatly planned;
When it's time for Jasper Sly to pass
He's going to singe *his* flaming arse!

* * *

FRED

Whilst standing one day on his head
An agile musician named Fred
Played Bach's Oboe Concerto,
But he said that it hurt so
He played one by Mozart instead.

GUS

A group of us helped our friend Gus
And his euphonium on to a bus.
Just imagine the glares
When it jammed in the stairs
Plus the fuss Gus thus thrust upon us.

BACH

Johann Sebastian Bach
Wrote much of his work in the dark
For Frederic Handel
Would blow out his candle
Night after night, for a lark

THE FLUTIST

It is dangerous playing the flute
With a top lip that's very hirsute
And the longer the whiskers
The greater the risk is
Of pulling them out by the root.

* * *

CONSCIENCE

Dear Mr Tax Man, The reason I write
Is my conscience is stopping me sleeping at night.
For a good many years now in every Return
I have grossly deflated the income I earn,
Thereby increasing the earnings I keep
But sadly reducing the hours that I sleep.

To ease my conscience I'm enclosing my cheque
For £5,000 which should have the effect
Of demonstrating my sincere contrition
And hopefully restoring my sleeping condition.
I'll give it a couple of weeks to restore
But then, if it hasn't, I'll send you some more.

* * *

THE RAIL-STRIKE

Len Bradshaw had fought tooth and nail
To be top dog at British Rail,
Forging a fearsome reputation
As one who'd brook no disputation.
But he'd met his match in Ronald Ross,
The tough, aggressive union boss,
As they fought each other every day
On the prickly point of extra pay.

Their dispute, of long duration,
Had lately failed at arbitration,
So Ronald, forced by malcontents,
Had called a strike for three weeks hence,
Which was a very grave mistake,
The sort that people sometimes make
Which, unforeseen, transforms their lives,
And in addition those of their wives.

Though adversaries business-wise
Ron and Len had family ties,
For Ron's wife, Jane, and Len's wife, Pat,
Were bosom friends, but more than that,
Ron was due to lead his daughter
Proud and fatherly t'wards the altar
To wed Len's son on that same day
As the railway strike got under way.

.

The wives, aghast to hear the news,
Could not believe that Ron would choose
To hold one union paramount,
But a family one of less account.
How that date slipped Ron's attention
Lay well beyond their comprehension.

By contrast, their whole concentration
Had focussed on the preparations
For their offsprings' coming wedding.
So seeing the way things now were heading
They planned to sort their men out first,
For left to them they feared the worst.

And so, as Ron approached his house
He met the force of his furious spouse.
"What were you thinking? You're Union-mad!
You'd think they're the only family you had.
That's the very same day our girl will wed,
Or did that fact not enter your head?

"You must think her wedding day
Should, on no account, get in the way
Of your Union's machinations!
But what about your blood-relations?
As you escort her along the aisle
Will you be thinking of your rank and file?
And in the vestry, about to sign,
Will you be standing in some picket line?
You've got to get your priorities right,
So get the strike called off – tonight!"

"I couldn't do that, Jane, without losing face,
And furthermore it would be a disgrace
To cave in to that Railway Board.
I'd be branded a traitor, a turncoat, a fraud."

In Len's house, too, the scene was fraught,
As Pat told her husband what exactly she thought.
"It's a pity that you, as the railway's voice,
Left Ron with no alternative choice
Than to call a strike, which I'm galled to say
Threatens our own son's wedding day.
The bitter irony will not be lost
"Upon the Press who, to our cost,

Will portray you two, linked by marriage,
With an idle, empty railway carriage.
We will become a laughing-stock,
Held up for the travelling public to mock.
So this dispute must be ended swiftly.
Why can't you both settle for fifty/fifty?"

Though feigning to be much perturbed,
In Len's mind just one thought recurred –
If Ron caved in, as he thought he must,
The Union's case would turn to dust.
"It's not that I'm bolshie. No, perish the thought,
But it's up to the Union. The ball's in their court."
For two more days the battle raged on,
With Pat lashing Leonard, and Jane bashing Ron.
But the men were intent upon settling a score,
Turned into a crisis from three days before.

Next day, in part to calm herself,
Jane took a book from the library shelf.
It was not a book one often sees -
A play by Aristophanes -
Penned during Athens' war with Sparta,
And simply entitled 'Lysistrata'.
In it the eponymous heroine
Had just devised a devious scheme -
She told the married women of Greece
That if they really wanted peace
And bring an end to the dreadful war
Then they should all forthwith withdraw
Their conjugal services from the men
Until they all saw sense again.

All of the wives took turns to speak,
And as one of them said in vernacular Greek,
"If you can't knock sense into a husband's head,
Then aim somewhere lower down instead!"

Jane read the play from beginning to end
Then rushed away to tell her friend
That in this play there lay the key
To unlock their husbands' obstinacy.

"Our curtain-lectures have utterly failed,
Despite the fact that we've earnestly railed
Against our husbands who, for personal pride,
Refuse to help set the strike-call aside.
Our words will not move them, try as we might,
So the only choice left is to stand up and fight.
That is the reason I think it's smarter
To follow the lead of Lysistrata.

"I know that it would truly vex
Our husbands thus deprived of sex,
But it may concentrate their minds
On feelings of another kind.

"Although our love-life will be inactive
We must take care to keep attractive
To remind them both of what they're missing –
The cuddles, the huddles, the intimate kissing;
Be subtly perfumed but not too glamorous,
Just enough to make them feel amorous;
Wear clothing highlighting our feminine curves
To gradually weaken their manly reserves."

The men heard their terms, leaving both of them winded –
Loving was off till the strike was rescinded!
In vain the two men wheedled and pleaded,
But all of their pleas went completely unheeded.
They gave them red roses by the score,
With suppliant taps on the bedroom door;
But in spite of all their billing and cooing
The result was always - nothing doing!

Sleeping alone and feeling frustrated,
Their firm resolution slowly abated
Till, after some days of night-starvation,
They faced the truth of their situation.
Having reached the end of their tether
The two men decided to meet together
To settle for good their industrial spate
And so bring an end to their celibate state.

Said Len, "You can say whatever you like,
It's up to your Union to call off this strike.
You know that our offer is just and fair.
There's no more cash that we can spare."
Said Ron, "It is rubbish, the things you say,
When I consider your directors' pay.
The Union's not where the onus lies –
It's there in your boardroom, bonus-wise."

"Enough! Enough! There's no point in bickering
When the light of our love-lives is barely flickering.
If this wedding is spoiled then it's perfectly plain
That our kids won't speak to us ever again.
This flaming dispute must be brought to an end!
It's driving us both around the bend!
I've had no nookie for more than a week,
And all because of some ancient Greek!"

"You don't have to tell me. You're not alone.
I, too, live in a nookie-free zone.
I must confess that I'm filled with longing
As amorous memories return a-thronging,
And my mounting level of testosterone
Refuses to leave my libido alone."

"I miss her smile, her elegant style,
Though I'm still not forgetting her devilish guile."
"I miss her fashion, her breath-taking passion,
Which incidentally she's trying to ration."

"I miss her zest, her humorous jests,
And I can't stop picturing her wondrous breasts."

"Those eyes!"
"Those sighs!"
"Those thighs!
"That prize!"

"Why are we torturing ourselves like this?
When back there at home there is kiss after kiss
Just waiting for this affair to be sorted,
And for us to say that the strike's been aborted.
It's clear neither you nor I will budge
So let us resort to the time-honoured fudge -
A vacuous clause on productivity,
So we each then can claim some sort of victory."

Next day both men faced the camera crews
And made their statement on the BBC News
"Uppermost in our minds throughout
The national interest has stood out.
Now, thanks to our efforts, it can truly be said
That all of our problems have been put to bed."

The wedding reception was a great success
With the guests and the media duly impressed.
Facing the multitudinous cameras
The two wives looked extremely glamorous,
Each dressed in the most exquisite style,
Each wearing an enigmatic smile.

So with ultimate feminine power asserted
The national rail-strike had been averted,
And, just as the chastened men assumed,
Normal service was duly resumed.

* * *

MARK ANTONY IN ROME

Friends, Romans, Countrymen, lend me your ears;
I come to bury Caesar, not to praise him.
The evil that men do lives after them;
The good is oft interred with their bones;
So let it be with Caesar.   The noble Brutus
Hath told you that Caesar was ambitious:
If it were so, it was a grievous fault,
And grievously hath Caesar answer'd it.
Here, under leave of Brutus and the rest –
For Brutus is an honourable man;
So are they all, all honourable men –
Come I to speak in Caesar's funeral.
He was my friend, faithful and just to me:
But Brutus says he was ambitious;
And Brutus is an honourable man.
He hath brought many captives home to Rome,
Whose ransoms did the general coffers fill:
Did this in Caesar seem ambitious?
When the poor have cried, Caesar hath wept;
Ambition should be made of sterner stuff:
Yet Brutus says he was ambitious;
And Brutus is an honourable man.
You all did see that on the Lupercal
I thrice presented him the kingly crown,
Which he did thrice refuse: was this ambition?
Yet Brutus says he was ambitious;
And, sure, he is an honourable man.
I speak not to disprove what Brutus spoke,
But here I am to speak what I do know.
You all did love him once, not without cause:
What cause withholds you then, to mourn for him?
O judgment! Thou art fled to brutish beasts,
And men have lost their reason. Bear with me;
My heart is in the coffin there with Caesar,
And I must pause till it come back to me.

Julius Caesar, Act III, Scene ii.

MARK ANTONY ON TOUR

Penge, Rodean, Cumberland, Tenby Broadstairs;
Pyecombe to Cirencester, not to Preston.
Yeovil Khatmandu Leeds Altrincham;
The Lowestoft Entebbe with Cologne;
So Wetherby with Pisa. Grenoble Luton
Hath Corfu that Pisa was Mauritius:
If it Thurso, it was St Peter Port,
And Peterlee hath Pisa Arlesford it.
Here, Sunderland of Luton Bucharest -
For Luton is a Barnstaple man;
So Hardwick Hall, all Barnstaple men -
Mumbai to Pekin Pisa's Liverpool.
He was Land's End, Bristol and Tuscany;
But Luton says he was Mauritius;
And Luton is a Barnstaple man.
He hath Portmeiron Cardiffs home to Rome,
Whose Grantham did the Jedburgh Huddersfield.
Widnes in Pisa seem Mauritius?
When Jaipur Strathclyde, Pisa Morpeth:
Cambodia should Belgrade of Dusseldorf:
Yet Luton says he was Mauritius;
And Luton is a Barnstaple man.
Ewell Pitsea that on the Kiel Canal
I Guiseley Tenterden a Camden Town
Wheathampstead Syracuse: was this Alfriston?
Yet Luton says he was Mauritius;
Pershore, he is a Barnstaple man.
I Didcot to Peru what Basingstoke,
But here Vietnam to Didcot Idaho.
Ewell did Dublin once, Niagara Falls:
Vauxhall Cotswolds you then, to Warlingham?
O Plumstead! Stourhead to Cowdenbeath,
And men have Gloucester Beeston. Becontree;
Stuttgart is in Wisconsin there with Pisa,
And Ullapool till it Trincomalee.

Puglia Pisa, Ajax 3, Spurs 2

THE V.I.P.

Last week she felt that she could cry,
That life, somehow, had passed her by.
At Cambridge she had trained to be
Important in society;
But her ambitions came to naught
When others needed her support.
Remembering just how great a feat
It always took to make ends meet,
It angered her how some folk earn
A quite ridiculous return.
With husband dead and children gone,
Steeped in self-pity she brooded on
The chances she'd been forced to miss.
And all for what? To end like this?

Then four soft words, a tiny hand,
Awakened her to understand -
Not every life is crowned with fame,
But all have value, just the same.
Just four dear words!
No wild acclaim,
No meteoric rise to fame,
No accolade bestowed on man,
Could match those words,
"I love you, Gran!"

What fools they are who quantify
Success by just how high they fly!
Let eagles soar the whole day long!
She'd rather hear the blackbird's song.

* * *

JOYCE THE VERGER

Joyce, the verger of a church nearby,
Hung out her monogrammed smalls to dry,
But then a wind of gale-force nine
Snatched the undies from off the line,
Whisking them to the vicarage lawn
Where they were discovered the following morn.

Two busy-body vigilantes
Scrutinised the bra and panties,
And, seeing t he verger's clear initials,
Promptly told the church officials.
Soon the air was filled with rumours
(Re the aforesaid dainty bloomers)
Of Joyce disporting at the vicar's,
Sans shame, sans bra, sans frilly knickers,
Revealing her unbridled lust
And rather well-developed bust.

The mounting scandal reached the ears
Of Bishop Bob who, gripped by fears
Of witches' covens, pagan rites,
Sexual orgies, Walpurgis nights,
Expressed himself extremely shocked;
And so the vicar was de-frocked.

Joyce now bore the vicious brunt
Of this malicious witches' hunt,
Enduring taunts and ostracism,
And quite unfounded criticism.
But then it quietly dawned on Joyce
That she in fact possessed a choice -
To suffer unfair banishment
Or merit unjust punishment.
In short, if one's to do the time,
One may as well enjoy the crime.

So, wearing sexy bra and knickers,
Joyce set off for the de-frocked vicar's,
Initiating a happy merger
Twixt innocent priest and vilified verger.
Ensconced in their conjugal bliss
The wagging tongues they do not miss,
But nightly bless the happy day
Her nether garments blew away.

* * *

TO THE BUMP

We're to share the same birthday, you and I,
Though they're eighty six years apart;
So just as I'm nearing my final good-bye
Your journey's preparing to start.

I expect I shall see you beginning to crawl
And later, when learning to stand,
And if ever I see you're about to fall
I'll put out a steadying hand.

Perhaps I'll be there as you lose your milk teeth
Or later, when wearing a brace,
Though if you don't have to I'll see the relief
Expressed on your pretty young face.

I'm trying to picture your first party dress.
Is it pink or a mixture of greens?
Or will you decide there's no need to impress
And turn up looking lovely in jeans?

I hope there'll be time to tell you some tales
Of the fairies two little girls knew,
Of goblins in Wales who steal guineapigs' tails,
For *my* tales are invariably true.

I'll do all I can to still be around
To learn of your progress at school,
And be present to hear the riotous sound
When you and your friends play the fool.

You'll have to excuse me if I can't be there
To witness your walk down the aisle,
To hear the onlookers truly declare
You're the loveliest bride by a mile.

As I told your dear Mum on her wedding day
I'm not one for giving advice,
But I trust when your Dad comes to give you away
It's to somebody equally nice.

But if you're *not* born on my coming birthday
Would that matter a lot, or a little?
For myself, hand on heart, I can honestly say,
Not a scrap, not a jot or a tittle,

The tie that connect us is fashioned to be
Firmly fixed and perpetually strong,
For you're a fresh bud on the family tree
And I'm just a few twigs along.

* * *

WATER CRISIS

"Simkins, you're my Special Adviser
So give me some special advice."
(It wasn't he thought Simkins wiser,
Just the best he could get at the price).

"We've got a severe water crisis.
The water's exceedingly low
In the Cherwell, the Mole and the Isis;
And the Piddle's not much of a flow.

"We can't wash our cars on the forecourts;
The brewers can't water the beer;
There's even talk at the Law Courts
That liquidations could soon disappear.

"There's a hosepipe ban for the garden;
There are standpipes out in the street.
The judges are reluctant to pardon
Those who'll not drink whisky neat.

"We're losing the floating voters.
They're deserting our banner in floods.
And even the week-end boaters
Are nothing but stick-in-the-muds.

"There are vicious suggestions, and spiteful,
That golf- and race-courses be hit.
They're resisted of course in Whitehall,
But let's face it, it could come to it.

"It could even affect Royal Ascot,
Though Heaven no doubt will forfend.
We'd better use Noah as our mascot,
For Lord knows how it will end.

"The PM is going bananas,
The Cabinet are doing their nuts.
They say they'll accept no mañanas,
No ifs and no water butts.

"So, Simkins, we've got to do something
To counter this terrible drought;
So get all your brain cells a'pumping
Before news of our panic leaks out."

Simkins' thoughts came in a trickle
From whatever passed as his brain
Which was noted for being quite fickle
On a subject as fluid as rain.

"I've got it," he cried with great fervour,
"It's not water-tight yet, of course;
But to make all the water go further,
Why don't we dilute it at source?"

"Simkins, my lad, you astound me!
And to think people say you are wet!
With such Special Advisers around me
I'll become the Prime Minister yet!"

* * *

THE WAKE

Certainly all the family knew
That Aunt Jane had a bob or two,
Which was, no doubt, as I contended,
Why her funeral was attended
By distant relatives by the dozens,
Including many dubious cousins
I never even knew existed,
Whose only interest there consisted
Of hoping to evaluate
What they might get from her estate.

The service over, we made our way
To Aunt Jane's house where, sad to say,
What should have been a friendly throng
Became a free-for-all ere long,
Which started when a favourite niece
Took the clock from the mantelpiece
And calmly put it in a bag,
Which clearly got Aunt Mary's rag.
"Jane promised me that clock!" she cried.
"Get lost!" the niece unladylike replied,
Then, spying Aunt Jane's golden locket,
Calmly slipped it in her pocket.

That seemed to be the starting gun
For others to join in the fun,
For, following a deathly hush,
There then occurred a headlong rush,
Which I suspect had long been planned,
To seize whatever lay at hand,
As nephews, cousins, aunts and nieces
Laid claim to various bits and pieces,
Vases, trinkets, figurines,
Silverware and soup tureens,
Plates and pictures from the walls
Leading to some vicious brawls,
While the fight for the cutlery canteen
Was the dirtiest scrap I've ever seen.

The rampage journeyed up the stair
Leaving us in deep despair,
As relatives in quick succession
Helped themselves to Aunt's possessions.
I felt as if our eyes were focussed
On to a ravenous swarm of locusts.
So shocked were we at what we saw
We felt that we could take no more,
And so without a backward glance
We took the first appropriate chance
To quit that scene of wanton pillage
And drove away from Aunt Jane's village,
Enraged and ranting at the way
Those relatives had caused a day
Which should have been of sad reflection
To veer off in a mad direction.

What sorrowed us the most by far
Was in unloading from our car
We accidentally dropped the Dyson
And smashed Aunt Jane's few bits of Meissen.

* * *

EMILY IS ONE

The birth of sweet Emily Victoria
Occasioned great family euphoria
And now that she's one
This bundle of fun
Makes my view on old age even sorrier.

* * *

TO BUMP No.2

I saw your clear image today, sweet girl,
Slumbering, secure and serene,
Patiently waiting for time to unfurl
Before you can to enter the scene.

It will be Springtime before we two meet,
You keen to blossom and bloom,
And me but a bald and bewhiskered old git
Sat bridling in God's waiting room.

What would we talk about, given the time,
Which I fear is proceeding apace?
I'd love to tell you some stories sublime
To bring smiles to your lovely young face.

I'd tell you the tale of a wicked old witch
With a wart on the tip of her nose.
She sneezed so hard it fell into a ditch –
Where it went to now nobody knows.

Or the elf who loved feasting on dairy ice-cream,
Like a balloon growing fatter each day.
But he sat on a thorn and with many a scream
Squirted onwards and upwards away.

Or the gnome who created a somnolent sound
Sending animals back to bed early;
But the sound turned the piglets around and around,
Which explains why their tails are so curly.

I hope I'll have time to tell you my views
On the rôle of the family bond
As the source from which all true worth ensues
Throughout our short life and beyond

Your parents will lovingly guide you along
Whichever path you decide
And if I'm not present to join in their song
In spirit I'll share in their pride.

Now you're to be born with the coming of Spring,
England's orchards approaching full bloom.
It's Earth's annual invitation to sing
Farewell to the past winter's gloom.

The bloom of the cherry's beyond dispute
And the worth of the pear's plain to see,
But the best of all blooms and the finest of fruit
Are found here on our family tree.

* * *

THE CELLIST

Whilst playing in front of the Queen
A cellist went suddenly green.
He could tell from her eyes
That the zip of his flies –
(but the rest of this poem's obscene).

THE BASSOONIST

My uncle who played the bassoon
Found it hard to remember the tune
So each night in bed
On the top of his head
He would tap out the beat with a spoon.

THE PIANIST

A fervent young pianist named Lucy
Was a passionate fan of Debussy.
When she played his 'La Mer'
Her audience's hair
Stood on end, and their flesh became goosey.

THE ACCORDIONIST

An extrovert lady from Bude
Once played the accordion nude
But her very first squeeze
Brought her straight to her knees
And her very next words were quite rude.

* * *

THE BIGAMIST

This is the tale of Peter Penny
Who married several wives too many
And finally was duly brought
Before the Matrimonial Court,
Charged with that most heinous crime
Of having far too good a time.

His many wives then hurried thence
To testify in his defence.
Unversed in tortuous litigation
They pressed the case for mitigation,
Using all their feminine arts
To melt the hardness of the judge's heart.
They pleaded they'd spend lonely nights
Deprived of their conjugal rights
With all the misery that entailed
Should darling husband Pete be jailed.

They sobbed that all their tiny tots
Would cry there waiting in their cots
For Pete to make his evening rounds
To read to them, by leaps and bounds,
Picking up each story's thread
From the point that he'd last read,
To kiss in turn each one goodnight
Before decamping in the night.
Could any judge be so cold-hearted
He'd see Dad and kiddies cruelly parted?

Next week, they wept, they'd planned to be
At Pete's next wedding ceremony
Where they would all be maids-of-honour;
But not if Peter were a goner.
They'd helped embroider the new bride's train.
Was all their needlework to prove in vain?

Seeing the tears that they were shedding
At the prospect of Pete's next wedding
Being scuppered by the Law,
The judge felt he could bear no more.
So he reviewed the evidence
And looked for legal precedents,
Then having searched for them in vain
He found Pete guilty - but insane,
Slyly ordering for good measure
That he be detained at his many wives' pleasure.

* * *

SPELLING TROUBLE

I often feel embarrassed that I can't spell words like harassed,
And at school I found the English lessons hell.
I was made to count the 's's in addresses and possesses
And the 'l's in parallelogram as well.
I had to use mnemonics to spell words like histrionics,
And vicissitude I never did attempt.
So while others left the college with encyclopaedic knowledge
My solecisms merited contempt.

Then last week when I felt queer with recurrent diarrhoea
My ipecacuanha brought on visions -
From my dog-eared OED buzzed a vicious spelling-bee
Citing words with somewhat silly definitions.

Diaeresis (those two dots); impetigo (nasty spots);
Iridescent; supersede and dynamism;
Proceedings (courts of law) and preceding (gone before);
Quarrelling and barrenness and schism;
Caduceus (Hermes' wand); larvae (creatures found in ponds);
Reconnaissance; recognisance and scion;
Hieroglyphics (from the Nile); nuclear physics (from the pile);
Ophthalmoscope (a thing to keep your eye on).

Miscellaneous words galore he spewed out as ne'er before,
Making him appallingly irascible.
Then when he reached zoology, in the name of etymology
He demanded I improve as soon as possible.
And so I acquiesced before my brain cells coalesced,
And naively promised him I'd concentrate
On learning how to spell tricky words like bagatelle,
Though I don't expect to shine or even scintillate.

There is one consolation to assuage my perturbation,
Which occasions wicked xenophobic glee -
The new translatory panel of our partners 'cross the Channel
If the truth be told are more nonplussed than me!

* * *

NICOLA NIXON

This is the tale of Nicola Nixon
Who suffered from a strange affliction
Which left her love life cruelly blighted,
Her sexual yearnings unrequited.

Whilst studying at the conservatoire
She'd built up such a repertoire
Her mind was filled to over-flowing
With tunes she whistled without knowing.

So while other girls when making love
Might coyly cast their eyes above
Or sigh or croon to indicate
Their feelings to their steady date,

Nicky, in the throes of passion,
Would in disconcerting fashion
Purse her lips and start to whistle,
Which rightly made her lovers bristle.

I mean, it really comes to this:
In moments of exceeding bliss
Who would willingly endure
A Richard Wagner overture.

And what perspiring enamorado
Would fancy tunes from The Mikado
Whistled shrilly in his ear
As the moment of great joy drew near?

Successive boy friends came and went
Much to her disgruntlement,
For even snogging in the parlour
Entailed a burst of Gustav Mahler.

No lover could maintain his urge
To the notes of Handel's funeral dirge.
The sad effect 'pon those who heard 'em
Was reductio ad absurdum.

All this made her recognise
That her strange quirk could jeopardise
Her happiness for years to come,
So she confided in her Mum.

Her dear Mama had somewhere read
That patriotic girls in bed
Lay back and thought of England, so
Should she not give that scheme a go?

Her Spanish beau was thus amazed
To hear, as in her eyes he gazed,
A rousing version of Rule Britannia
And a chorus or two of Viva Espana.

In desperation now she turned
To a man whom she discerned
Would tolerate her more than most,
Since he was deafer than a post.

Now in confidence she lay
Until he stole it all away,
Wondering as he checked his pace
Why she was blowing in his face.

But Cupid solved her awkward poser
By sending her a young composer
Who wrote her many a composition
With tempi geared to her condition.

He now attends her concerts nightly
Concentrating eruditely
Upon her handling of the score,
Favoured at times by a glad encore.

SADLY MISSED

He felt or sensed her footstep on the stair,
Accompanied by the rustle of her gown,
And her delicate perfume
Seemed to permeate the room –
But, alas, his wishful thinking let him down.

Her absence seemed to drench the dismal air
As he recalled their moment of goodbye.
She had said, "I won't be long",
Kissed his cheek, and then was gone,
Leaving him alone to ask the question, "Why?"

Time had since dragged more than he could bear
As he, bereft of purpose, sat alone.
Could he but have her back
There was nothing she would lack,
And for all his past shortcomings he'd atone.

He plumped the cushion on her favourite chair
And eyed the clock upon the mantel shelf –
Already well past noon –
So unless she came back soon
He would have to put the kettle on himself.

* * *

GREEK HISTORY IN VERSE

On Homer

I think a diploma
Is due to old Homer
For his epic account of the Iliad.
Fate was very unkind,
For they say he was blind;
Which shows what a very strong wiliad.

On the Iliad

After fighting for ten years at Troy
The Achaeans weren't having much joy;
So they built a huge horse,
Filled with soldiers, of course,
An ingenious and match-winning ploy.

On Greek Historians

Herodotus, Thucydides and Xenophon
Are the ones we are bound to rely upon.
Were it not for their histories
We'd be faced with great mysteries,
And no one would now run the marathon.

On the Persian Invasion

While playing the Greeks at monopylae
Xerxes arrived at Thermopylae.
He couldn't pass 'Go'
For a fortnight or so,
So he sneaked round the back - quite impropylae.

But you cannot dishearten
A disciplined Spartan,
So they took this reverse in their stride.
Though completely surrounded
They remained unconfounded
And fought till the last man had died.

On Xerxes

Unaware of the Athenian fleet,
Xerxes settled himself on his seat;
But there wasn't a trace
Of a smile on his face
As he witnessed his utter defeat.

On Pericles

Pericles, or so it is said,
Was endowed with a very large head.
He had the good sense
To cut back on defence
And rebuild the city instead.

On Alcibiades

Some talk of Alexander
And some of Hercules;
But for brazen cheek
My favourite Greek
Is Alcibiades.

On the Peloponnesian War

The Peloponnesian War
Lasted longer than Athens foresaw.
Already begun
In four-thirty-one
It ended BC four-o-four

The war in the Peloponnese
Brought Athens at last to her knees;
Which was a great pity
For no other city
Acquired such a talent to please.

On Greek intellectuals

Archimedes invented the screw.
Pythagoras was quite clever too.
And I dare say a lotle
Think old Aristotle
Deserves a fair mention or two.

On Aristophanes

The hard-hitting taunts that one ophanses
In the plays of Aristophanes
Were designed to deflate
The rich and the great
So he made no attempt to sophanthes.

On the Sacred War

Instead of paying wages
To their prophets, seers and sages,
They gave them gold and silver gifts galore;
So the oracle at Delphi
Became extremely welphi
And its treasure brought about the Sacred War.

On Philip II

'He's having the time of his life!'
Cried Philip of Macedon's wife.
'Having conquered all Greece
He's now bedding my niece!'
So she just cut him dead - with a knife.

On Alexander

While still little more than a lad
Alexander succeeded his dad.
Eschewing inertia
He conquered all Persia,
Turning back when he reached Hyderabad.

On Reflection

So ends this brief history in verse.
Though not clever it could have been worse.
Be glad I don't speak
Vernacular Greek,
And my stanzas, though tortured, are terse.

* * *

TONY

"I'm prepared to be judged by God," Tony said,
Displaying precipitate valour.
"For his back he has fashioned a rod," said Ahmed.
"I don't fancy his chances with Allah."

*

DISCORDANCE.

Many a modern composition
Benefits from this condition –
Whenever a note is wrongly struck,
With just a modicum of luck
Few would spot the imprecision.

* * *

RALPH (1922-2006)

He held out his hand at the rugby stand
To accept the Inter-Schools Shield;
But the rumble of war would soon slam the door
On the dreams of the teams on the field.

Chorus: *Some moved straight to manhood, by-passing*
youth,
So lessening their chance to grow long in the
tooth.

They walked hand in hand from the bridge to the
Strand
As the planes thrummed in menace above.
Each promised to wait on the outcome of fate,
And do nothing to tarnish their love.

Chorus: *The end for some couples, in love when they*
parted,
Would be one racked by guilt, and one broken-
hearted.

He received a big hand back in Bomber
Command
On the day he received his commission.
Then he and his crew courageously flew
On many a flak-ridden mission.

Chorus: *Despite their great losses, their courage and*
pain,
No medal was struck to mark their campaign.

He held out his hands, his proud caring hands,
To cradle his newly-born son.
For him and his wife this gift of new life
Meant their own lives had truly begun.

Chorus: *By Nature all parents are strictly mandated*
To love and to cherish the young they've created.

He bowled underhand to his son on the sand,
With his wife keeping wicket behind.
In his mind he could see a fine young man-to-be,
Unaware that his mind's-eye was blind.

Chorus: *It's best not to know what lies just ahead.*
            "Count no man happy until he is dead".

He flung out his hand to prevent the act planned
By his son in the depths of despair;
But the deed had been done, and his dearly-loved son
Now lay crumpled beyond human care.

Chorus: *Anguish can pierce one up to the hilt,*
            With a mixture of sorrow, shame, blame and
            guilt.

He offered his hand to the unhappy band
Of young men in the vice of addiction,
And year after year, for the cause he held dear,
He restored their lost pride and conviction.

Chorus: *A painting discoloured by varnish and grime*
            Can with patient endeavour be returned to its
            prime.

He lifted her hand, her cold lifeless hand,
And brought it once more to his lips.
Now completely alone, all happiness flown,
His world seemed in total eclipse.

Chorus: *One must have time to grieve but recognize too*
            That life does go on; there is work still to do.

He held out his hand by royal command
To receive the great honour awarded.
If they could but see, how delighted they'd be
To see his life's work so rewarded.

Chorus: *Though volunteers work with no payment in mind,*
Recognition does soften a very hard grind.

A mysterious hand which he could not withstand
Now ushered him gently from life.
He'd shake hands anew with his team-mates, his crew,
His dearly-loved son and his wife.

Chorus: *Death is naught but a restful and undisturbed sleep.*
But the memories one sows are what others will reap.

* * *

FLY-LEAF DEDICATIONS

To the Twins

This book is owned jointly by both of the Twins,
Which means that an ownership dialogue begins,
For if it's just one book that's owned by the pair,
Which part can each of them claim as her share?
Does Hope own the bottom half and Mallory the top?
Start thinking this way and where does one stop?
Apportioning it physically is clearly quite risible.
A book by its nature is indivisible.
One can't tear a book apart straight down the middle,
So I must endeavour to sort out the riddle.

Could Hope own it weekdays and Mallory weekends?
Or based on the reading time each of them spends?
One can picture the disputes, the aggro, the scowls,
If Hope owns the consonants and Mallory the vowels.
And if Hope owns the verbs and Mallory the nouns
The status of gerunds would cause a few frowns.
Dear Lord! What a problem, but I think I have found
A solution you girls will find perfectly sound.
You'll share the book sweetly, like peas in a pod.
Hope owns the even pages, Mallory the odd.

By checking your pages, Twins, you'll be happy to see
That they're just as inseparable as you'll always be.

*

To Emily

With more love
Than there are
Stars
In the sky

*

To Isabella

With more love
Than there are
Pebbles
On the shore

*

To Jack

With more love than
The pink and purple pimples on a pound of pickled pork,
Plus the tens of tortured tutors teaching tortoises to talk,
Plus the charms of cheeky children choosing chocolates to chew,
Plus the bowls of bubbling bacon broth bald barbers barbecue,
Plus the sounds of seasoned sausages set sizzling on the stove,
Plus the dark and dirty dustcarts duty dustmen duly drove,
Plus the crop of crusty croissants cruelly crumbling in the crypt,
Plus the wails of wanton wastrels waiting weekly to be whipped,
Plus the nicely knitted night shirts naked nudists never need,
All of which you will agree means lots of love indeed.

* * *

NARKOVER COLLEGE

As your teen-aged son's headmaster I must tell you, Mr. Blaster,
That his behaviour leaves a lot to be desired.
We encourage self-expression but he gives the firm impression
That many nods in that direction are required.

The graffiti which he scrawls on the nearby village walls
Is a constant source of obloquy and shame.
Though his words are always rude and his drawings very crude
His poor spelling gives the school a dreadful name.

He is selling marihuana at the college's gymkhana
Despite receiving very strict advice.
I fear that what he's doing will lead some boys to ruin
For he charges well above the current market price.

The liquor he distils in the chemistry lab stills
He is selling at the local leather works.
Whichever way you view it, it is wrong for him to do it,
For he knows full well that's the chemo master's perks.

I am told by Mrs. Sessions that he gives biology lessons
To her daughter in the pavilion after supper.
This is bad for discipline, as that daughter, Geraldine,
Is the mistress who's in charge of Vb Upper.

Worst of all he's spreading rumours about me and Mrs. Loomas
Which is causing me considerable unease.
I would have a lot to fear if her husband got to hear
When he gets home from serving overseas.

All in all I have concluded that he ought to be excluded
And yet I'd like to give him one more chance.
I would certainly much rather, with assistance from his father,
View his many misdemeanours more askance.

The thing I have in mind, is he's not been very kind
In besmirching Mrs. Loomas's good name.
But if you can guarantee that he'll end this calumny
I'll treat all his many scrapes as just a game.

Oh, splendid, Mr. Blaster! Now, as your son's headmaster
I can tell you teaching him has been a boon.
Now that we see eye to eye I can see no reason why
He shouldn't be school captain very soon.

* * *

OLD MRS WILLIAMS

"You are old, Mrs Williams," the young man said,
"And yet you're still gadding about.
Won't you slacken your pace
And grow old with the grace
Of those who fear time's running out?"

"I'm still full of life," Mrs Williams replied,
"And enjoy going out with my chums,
For experience has shown us
Each new day's a bonus,
So we take every one as it comes."

"You are grey, Mrs Williams," the young man declared,
"Many years from the first flush of youth.
Would you care to confess
That your fashionable dress
Is your way of concealing the truth?"

"Once you've learnt you're as young as you feel," she replied,
"Your dress-sense of old re-appears;
And I feel that I'm
Just approaching my prime -
And have been for forty odd years!"

"You are plump, Mrs Williams," the young man went on,
"And your shadow I fear's growing bigger.
Aren't you just a bit sad
All the chocolates you've had
Have put paid to your once-youthful figure?"

"Not at all!" Mrs Williams replied with a laugh,
"And although I'm aware of my thighs
I feel no distress
For I know M & S
Do cater for one further size."

"You are fun, Mrs Williams," the young man enthused,
"For I hear your gay laughter a lot.
Though you've many a wrinkle
Your eyes fairly twinkle.
Is it something you're taking, or what?"

"Away with you now!" Mrs W cried,
And she went back indoors with a grin,
Where she and her beau
Felt a warm inner glow
As they sipped the remains of her gin.

* * *

MR. v MRS.

"I have noticed, Mrs Whitely, that you're sleeping very lightly
And you toss and turn in bed at night as well.
Does the friend you're seeing nightly
Not prick your conscience slightly?
Is there anything that you would care to tell?"

"I can tell you, Mr Whitely, that the friend I visit nightly
Is depressed and therefore very far from well;
And my visits to her rightly
Are designed to make her sprightly
And to bring her out more quickly from her shell."

"I should tell you, Mrs Whitely, that I followed you there quietly,
In the moonlight saw you ring upon the bell,
And the one who hugged you tightly
And kissed you oh so lightly
Was a man as far as anyone could tell."

"I grant you, Mr Whitely, that my friend's physique is slightly
Larger than your average modern belle.
She always stands uprightly
And, the moon not shining brightly,
Could easily be mistaken for a swell."

"You are lying Mrs Whitely, for I know the fellow slightly;
He's the chap behind the bar at our hotel.
I can't treat this matter lightly,
And now tell you most forthrightly
That your duty as my wife I must compel!"

"I'm delighted, Mr Whitely, you now see the picture rightly,
For it now emboldens me to bid farewell.
I shall do so impolitely
And not the least contritely.
Unsightly Mr Whitely, go to hell!"

* * *

DREAMS FOR SALE

If there were dreams for sale
What would you buy?
Nothing's beyond the pale,
No price too high.

If there were dreams for sale
(Would that there were!)
I'd buy something priceless
Yet freer than air.
I once gaily owned some
Which seeped through my hands
Ending as grains upon
Life's golden sands.
If there were dreams for sale
TIME would I buy.

Were you to purchase Time
How would you spend
Those hours now made sublime
Till journey's end?

Were I to purchase Time
(How Hope unfurls!)
I'd follow the fortunes
Of two little girls.
I'd tell them some stories,
Some funny, some sad,
Showing some views of Life
Not always bad.
Were I to purchase Time
Thus would I spend.

Time's not for me to sell.
Time's running out
For your tales to tell.
Soon there'll be nowt.

If Time's not for you to sell
(Now things annoy!)
I'd write me a book or two
For them to enjoy.
Hearing the tales I'd tell
Though not at my knee
They'd sense behind my words
Something of me.
If Time's not for you to sell,
That must I do.

* * *

DORKING GIRLS

O give me a strapping young Dorking girl
With limbs as strong as young oaks;
A buxom and agile hill-walking girl
Who'd drink beer and recount bawdy jokes.
We'd wander the hillside together,
Letting the daylight hours pass.
She'd allow me to cushion my head on her bosom
And be jolly good fun in the grass.

O give me a brainy young Dorking girl
With a truly impressive IQ;
A veritable Stephen Hawking girl
Whose knowledge I'd gladly imbue.
We'd discuss quantum physics together,
The Arts and the heavens above;
And she would explain that her logical brain
Requires her to champion free love.

O give me a gorgeous young Dorking girl
Attending the College of Art;
A tall, absolutely corking girl
Who'd encourage me to take part.
We'd enrol in the life class together
Sketching each other quite nude;
But the methods we'd seek to improve our technique
Would not be approved by a prude.

O spare me, you nubile young Dorking girls;
My fantasies are causing me pain;
For if you were plain hideously squawking girls,
My wife would forbear to complain.
As it is, when we're shopping together
And she notices me glancing your way,
She gives me a dig in the side of my ribs,
And it hurts for the rest of the day.

* * *

DANIEL DOWD

This is the tale of the late Daniel Dowd,
A man excessively over-endowed
In the willy department, to put it politely;
Though the rest of this poem may get ruder – slightly.

Some of his neighbours will always remember
The problem caused by his unusual member
At the time of Daniel's untimely demise
Because of its very exceptional size.

For Daniel had died with a large erection,
Clearly visible from every direction,
Since it remained after rigor mortis had set in,
Which Kitty his wife found most upsetting.

As he lay on his back in the marital bed
A sheet covering his body, apart from his head,
Daniel had no possible chance of concealing
The mighty organ pointing up to the ceiling.

The sheet seemed to be determinedly hell-bent
On wishing to appear like a military bell-tent,
Complete apart from the usual vent-hole,
And held aloft by Dan's rigid tent pole

Kitty phoned Lovejoy, the local mortician,
To undertake the whole funeral commission.
He duly arrived with Eric, his mate,
A young lad two hinges short of a gate.

Seeing the tent as he entered the room,
The mortician sensed the deepening gloom.
Horizontal problems he'd solved in particular,
But never before, one so perpendicular.

He gave the tent-pole a powerful nudge,
Only to find that the thing didn't budge.
Even acknowledging Dan's rampant condition,
He hadn't expected such stiff competition.

They pulled back the sheet to discover the hitch
And seeing Dan lying without a stitch
They look'd at each other with a wild surmise –
Silent, upon a peek at Daniel's thighs.

Lovejoy grasped the tent-pole and using full force
Started to move it on a downward course.
He strained and grunted and by degrees
Brought it down level to below Daniel's knees.

Alas, he had failed in his strenuous mission,
For he'd merely brought Dan to a sitting position,
And when in astonishment he finally let go
Daniel reverted to the status quo.

Such problems weren't listed in the "Morticians' Manual"
Nor touched upon in the "Woodworkers' Annual",
So Lovejoy sighed and took out his tape
To take the measurements of Dan's inert shape.

"The width - that's OK. And so is the length.
Now for the height - may the Lord give me strength!
He'll not fit into any casket we make,
But we must think of something for poor Kitty's sake."

Eric thought hard and eventually cried,
"Let's lay him out proper, but on his right side!"
"That's merely transferring the bone of contention
Without success to another dimension.

"With the measurements we've got, however you view it,
And no matter how careful we are when we skew it,
It's going to take a senior wrangler
To fix the position of Dan's bobby-dangler."

"I've heard when a nurse is examining a chap
And he gets an erection, she gives it a rap
With the edge of her pencil and so very soon
It shrinks just like a deflated balloon."

"I'm sure that would work in a high percentage
Of cases involving a normal appendage,
But even a pencil as hard as 4H
Would have little effect in this present case."

"Why don't we just cut a hole in the lid
Then poke it through, but keep it well hid
With lots of large flowers tightly packed?
It could be a floral tribute, in fact."

"A floral tribute? I see what you mean
But if the flowers fell off, all would be seen.
Just imagine the cards that people could send –
"A Pillar of Strength", "Upright to the End""

"We could trim it off to make the lid level,"
Suggested the over-zealous young devil.
"Honestly, Eric! You're at it again!
You haven't thought about matching the grain!"

"We could say it's a knot in the wood," he persisted,
But Lovejoy just looked at him, grim and tight-fisted,
Surprised that the ignorant, uncouth little basket
Could suggest a knot for his top-o'-the-range casket.

"Perhaps Mrs Lovejoy could make a suggestion
On what to do with the willy in question?"
Eric naughtily asked with an innocent air,
But Lovejoy just gave him a withering glare.

The vicar arrived to pay his respects,
And, seeing the bell-tent, searched for a text.
"They were even hard at death's door" he quoted.
But quite out of context, let it be noted.

Now Lovejoy himself liked an apt quotation
And rapidly rose to meet the occasion.
"He's a problem must puzzle the devil." he said,
Which remark made the vicar swivel his head.

"Is he possessed, then?" he asked the mortician,
Who fast re-assessed his parlous position.
"I'm sure of it, Vicar. It's a strong possibility",
Thus passing the problem to Higher Authority.

"I must quickly arrange a service of exorcism,"
The vicar announced, "to avoid any criticism
That I'm not doing all that I can for my flock
Who have always appeared as firm as a rock."

The service was unusually well attended,
Though the notice was not what the vicar intended.
Lady parishioners were extremely surprised
To read that Dan's willy was to be exercised.

Despite the church service the bell-tent remained,
Leaving Kitty's unhappiness barely contained.
"What can I do now?" she asked sister, Tess.
"Which way can I turn to get out of this mess?"

"If his journey to the other side's been impeded
Then a medium's services are urgently needed.
It could very well be she'd be able to find
Whatever was preying on poor Daniel's mind."

Daniel's last thoughts were as plain as a pikestaff,
But Kitty reluctantly phoned Mrs Wagstaff
With no hope of success, and acutely aware
That a job well done by a medium is rare.

And so Mrs Wagstaff, forty and portly,
Commenced her séance, and indeed very shortly
Went into a trance, and with dulcet tone
Asked Dan to make his ethereal self known.

She told him she thought that it was a great pity
He'd died without saying goodbye to Kitty;
So was there something he wanted to say
To help brush her sorrow and anguish away?

After a pause she sat up with a start,
Aware of the quickening beat of her heart.
For quite a long time she sat rhythmically swaying,
Moving her lips as if silently praying.

She moaned at times, her plump body heaving,
Gasping for air and swiftly breathing.
Then she flung out her arms as if unable
To control herself, and grasping the table,

She arched her back with a cry supreme
And let out one final orgasmic scream.
Then with eyes closed she sat still for a while,
Her features enhanced by an impish smile.

She got up from the table, panting no more,
And made her way slowly towards the front door.
She turned and addressed the whole company at large,
"I'll see myself out, dears, and there'll be no charge."

"No charge indeed!" sister Tessa then cried.
"She didn't do anything!" But deep down inside
Kitty sensed that some very strange work was at play
And ran back upstairs to where Daniel lay.

The bell-tent had vanished, the tent-pole was gone,
And Daniel's complexion now radiantly shone.
Kitty held back her tears, kissed her warm fingertips,
Then tenderly laid them on Dan's smiling lips.

*

Arriving back home still flustered and red,
Mrs Wagstaff turned to her husband and said:
"As you very well know, Alf, I've been a good wife,
But now I need something more out of life.
Today at the séance without any urging,
I felt the free spirit within me surging,
Thus revealing, in spite of your boast,
That you need Viagra more than most."

*

On their way back to the Chapel of Rest
Lovejoy had something to get off his chest.
He turned to his young apprentice and said:
"You know, Eric, a thought has just entered my head.
The art of the medium, over centuries imparted,
Is raising the spirit of one dear departed;
But when there are unquenched passions to quell,
Mrs Wagstaff can lower the flesh as well."

*

That evening as the vicar lay back in his bed
He turned to his pretty young wife and said:
"I know that mediums can produce ectoplasm,
But today Mrs Wagstaff achieved ecto-orgasm."
Said she,"You believe it was genuine, I take it,
But can you be sure she didn't just fake it?"
"Oh no, dear" said he, "I'd have seen right through it."
"Really?" thought Joyce. "Well, I sometimes do it."

*

As Tessa was putting her case in the car
To journey back home to Leamington Spa
She turned to her sister Kitty and said:
"How will you cope now that Daniel is dead?"
"I know I'll have setbacks as never before,
But I'll keep his example well to the fore.
I'll square up to problems, not seeking evasion,
And rise, just like he did, to every occasion."

* * *

A VERY SAD TALE

It was Thursday, in The Cabin. I was queueing for my pension.
In front of me were two old dears whose talk caught my attention.
"And how's your Bill?" one of them asked. "I haven't seen him lately
Ambling 'cross the Common, which I know he values greatly."

A tear came to the other's eye. The subject caused her sorrow.
"My Bill is dead, I'm sad to say, three weeks ago tomorrow."
"Oh dear. I *am* surprised, for he seemed so fit, your Bill.
Did he have an accident? Did he suffer? Was he ill?"

"I'd just come back from shopping. I gets off the bus from Crawley.
I'd been as quick as I could be cos I knew that 'e felt poorly.
'I'm back', I calls. 'It's only me. I've something nice for supper'.
Then I goes into the kitchen. I was dying for a cuppa.

"I takes it to the living room; 'e's in 'is favourite chair.
I could tell from 'is expression 'e was downcast, full of care.
I puts my arm around 'im and I strokes 'is tousled 'ead.
'E looks at me, gives one long sigh and then slumps forward, dead!"

"Oh lawks! Why that was dreadful! What a shock that must have been!
You were alone. What did you do? Did you call for help, I mean?"
"I goes up to the telephone, and phones my brother, Ted.
'I've got bad news,' I says to 'im, 'My dear old Billy's dead.'

"'E says 'I'll come straight over. You leave everything to me.
I'll bury 'im in the garden where 'e always liked to be.'"
I stood there in astonishment, mouth open, eyes agog.
I can't be sure, but I like to think dear Billy was her dog.

* * *

A LIFE IN NINE STANZAS

Diary: nineteen forty six.
First see the light of day.
Cloth bound tightly round my tum.
Bottles, nappies, powdered bum,
My daily roundelay.

Diary: nineteen fifty eight.
Passed 11 plus. Hooray!
Bosoms growing. Facts of life.
Tears and tantrums. Problems rife.
Unhappy, come what may.

Diary: nineteen sixty four.
Am Cambridge bound today.
Dancing, socials, lectures too.
Wooed by many a hopeful Blue;
Kept all but one at bay.

Diary: nineteen seventy two.
Family on the way.
Broke but happy making do.
Hoping that all dreams come true
For two hearts young and gay.

Diary: nineteen eighty two.
Three kiddies out at play.
They're better now, but how I cried
When I thought the youngest one had died.
That's when I learnt to pray.

Diary: nineteen ninety one.
Huge school-fees to defray.
We're stretched and mortgaged to the hilt,
And often with a twinge of guilt
Resent how much we pay.

Diary: nineteen ninety eight.
Am widowed, sad to say.
Probate. Pension. Taxes. Fees.
He used to deal with things like these.
Grandchildren often stay.

Diary: year two double oh four.
Have joined the U3A.
Meetings. Classes. Friendships, too.
A host of things that I can do.
No hardship being grey.

What plans have I for ten years hence?
In sunshine I'll make hay.
But if I'm gone, then - what the hell -
A stone somewhere will doubtless tell
I've quietly passed away.

* * *

HOME TRUTHS

You're wrong when you say I'm still balding,
That the treatment's not doing the trick,
For I saw in the mirror this morning
That the hair in my ears is quite thick.

How can you say that I'm fatter!
I'm slimmer than you care to think.
If you must have the truth of the matter –
These modern materials shrink.

You are cruel to say I'm forgetful;
That things just go out of my head,
So, far from my being regretful
I'm – Sorry, what was it you said?

It's not true I'm beginning to dawdle,
Less agile than I used to be.
It's just the old dear with the poodle
Was walking much faster than me.

What makes you say that I'm dozy?
It's seldom I take forty winks,
But when a room's peaceful and cosy
One relaxes .. maturely .. and thinks.

You don't have to tell me I'm past it.
I can work that one out for myself.
But I'm damn-well not due for a casket
Or an urn to be placed on some shelf.

* * *

INTELLIGENT DESIGN

The jagged pothole, during rain,
Became completely filled again
As myriad raindrops gaily surged
Into the rough-edged hole and merged.

I passed the very spot whilst walking
And clearly heard the raindrops talking.
I heard one cry, "Friends! Brothers! See!
This pothole fits us perfectly.
Though roughly shaped it is uncanny
How well we fit each nook and cranny.
'Tis plain why it was fashioned thus,
For it was surely made for us
By a hand which, from the start,
Has had our welfare at its heart."

I paused and wondered in my mind
Whether it would be unkind
To tell the raindrops what we know -
That far from being fashioned so,
What scars the surfaces of roads
Are lorries bearing heavy loads,
Whose drivers, far from wishing well,
Often cursed the rain which fell;
But when I voiced those thoughts aloud
They were abruptly disavowed.

In time the Council workmen came
To fill the pothole in again,
Working a summer's morning through
To make the surface smooth and true.
It soon was done, so now the rain
Goes gurgling gaily down the drain,
Too gay to give a second's thought
To the over-burdened juggernaut.

* * *

ELEGY

Think clearly, Mind,
lest I wander into night.
Gaze raptly, Eyes,
that I share a babe's delight.
Speak kindly, Lips,
lest remembrances be harmed.
Beat softly, Heart,
that old passions stay becalmed.
Touch gently, Hands,
lest your firmness causes pain.
Sing sweetly, Voice,
that some snatches may remain.
Tread slowly, Feet,
lest I reach too soon the end.
Strike cleanly, Death,
that I count you as a friend.
Judge lightly, Lord,
that I be a welcome guest.
Pass gaily, Friends,
when I'm duly laid to rest.

* * *

ABOUT THE AUTHOR

Ken Kelsey is a retired Barrister and Chartered Secretary and lives in Dorking. He has written three books of Number Puzzles brought together in an omnibus volume "The Ultimate Book of Number Puzzles" all published by Random House, and "A Beginner's Guide to Magic Squares and Cubes". He has also written a comic novel of life in a fictional English village in the 1950s entitled "The Nutcombe Papers" and an adventure story for young schoolgirls entitled "Sophie's Odyssey", both available from Amazon. He is one of the dwindling number of WW II code-breakers and is a founding member of the Dorking and District U3A.

* * *

30391507R00050

Printed in Great Britain
by Amazon